THE DETHRONEMENT OF TRUTH

THE DETHRONEMENT OF TRUTH

DIETRICH VON HILDEBRAND

HILDEBRAND
PROJECT

First Edition

Published 2021 by Hildebrand Press
1235 University Blvd., Steubenville, Ohio 43952

Publisher's Cataloging-in-Publication Information

Names: Von Hildebrand, Dietrich, 1889–1977, author.
Title: The dethronement of truth / Dietrich von Hildebrand.
Description: Steubenville, OH: Hildebrand Press, 2021.
Subjects: LCSH Truth. | Philosophy. | BISAC PHILOSOPHY / Essays | PHILOSOPHY / Ethics & Moral Philosophy
Classification: LCC BD171 .V64 2021 | DDC 121—dc23

ISBN: 978-1-939773-18-0
LCCN: 2021923363

The Hildebrand Project is grateful to acknowledge Stanley and Penny Sienkiewicz, whose generous support made possible the publication of this book.

Set in Monotype Perpetua, a typeface designed by English sculptor Eric Gill
Typeset by Kachergis Book Design

Front Cover Font: Hoefler Text
Cover Image: The Burning of the Houses of Lords and Commons, 16 October 1834, by J. M. W. Turner, in the Cleveland Museum of Art
Image Source: Wikimedia Commons, Public Domain

Production and Cover Design by Christopher T. Haley

www.hildebrandproject.org

CONTENTS

THE DETHRONEMENT OF TRUTH

One of the most ominous features of the present epoch is undoubtedly the dethronement of truth. In former times, whatever might have been professed, doctrines were always put forward with the claim that they were true. All theories, however erroneous and absurd their content might have been, appealed always to the question of truth as to the ultimate, decisive judge. From the very beginning of our occidental culture, all errors were propagated in the name of truth. The question of whether something was true or not was taken very seriously, and even when the real motives for adhering to an error

This essay first appeared in 1943 in the Proceedings of the American Catholic Philosophical Association (Vol. XVII) and was later included in Hildebrand's collection of essays *The New Tower of Babel* (New York: Kennedy & Sons, 1953).

were unconsciously rooted in the will of the erring person, truth was acknowledged to be the supreme, ultimate judge of every theory.

Paradoxical as it may seem, even the various theories that denied objective truth or the possibility of knowing it, such as skepticism, relativism, agnosticism, were advanced in the name of truth. Lengthy books were written in order to prove that the denial of truth was irrefutable from the viewpoint of truth. No one hesitated to recognize truth as the ultimate judge, in spite of the fact that the proposed thesis denied objective truth. In denying truth, man appealed implicitly to truth.

Later on we shall deal with this blatant contradiction; here it suffices to state that every theory, ideology, and philosophy of life was professed under the banner of truth and that the seriousness of the question whether something was true or not was always recognized and respected.

It was the doubtful privilege of Communism and Nazism to dethrone truth for the first time by showing a complete indifference toward the question of whether something was true or not, and by replacing this question with subjective measures, such as the proletarian mentality in the former and the feeling of the Nordic race in the latter. The mutiny against the spirit embodied in Nazism testifies to this excommunication of truth from all the domains of life. Conformity to the feeling of the Nordic race or of the German people replaced every objective standard of truth, goodness, beauty, and right.

In 1933 the Bavarian minister of education, Mr. Schemm, declared solemnly before the assembled professors of the University: "From this day on, you will no longer have to examine whether something is true or not, but exclusively whether or not it corresponds to the Nazi ideology."

The climax of this ousting of the role of truth as supreme judge is to be found in paragraph 24 of the first official program of the Nazi party, stating that Christianity should be accepted to the extent that it is in agreement with the feeling of the Nordic race. Even concerning the ultimate sphere upon which the eternal fate of man depends, the question of the truth of its claims has lost its importance. In the past, martyrs died in order to give witness to the truth of Christianity. A great deal of blood was shed in wars fought in the name of religious truth. Heretics always claimed that they professed the one true religion. Atheists of former times took very seriously the question of the truth of God's existence, and they all agreed that truth alone had to determine man's religious creed. All their arguments against God's existence had the function of defending truth. Whatever their real motives, they accepted the necessity of appealing to truth as to the ultimate judge and the undisputed presupposition for any discussion. To make the question of whether one should accept or reject a religion depend upon the conformity to the feeling of the Nordic race—that is, upon a completely contingent and subjective standard—is a species of relativism unheard-of in all human history.

The same applies to Bolshevism or Communism. Every proposition uttered by Soviet propaganda has the character of a pure slogan, of a propaganda weapon; the meaning of words has been replaced with the emotional effect they are to create in the mind of the public. For instance, when Molotov speaks of the "eastern type of democracy," it is obvious that what he means is the very opposite of democracy; or when the Soviets manifest indignation over the lack of liberty in Franco's Spain, they ignore the fact that compared with their lack of freedom it is a *quantité négligeable*.

The most drastic symptom of the dethronement

of truth, however, is the way that contradictory opinions are accepted in submission to the command of the Politburo. Before 1938, Nazi Germany was characterized as an arrogant and criminal aggressor; from 1939 to 1941 the state was pictured as unjustly attacked by the vicious plutocratic nations. The fact that a state changes its attitude toward another is certainly not surprising; it is, rather, a very ordinary occurrence in politics. But it is a very unusual and surprising fact that no effort is made to explain how one judgment about a system and an ideology is replaced by an opposite judgment. That this transition takes place without any attempt to justify it reveals complete indifference toward the question of truth and the cynical dethronement of truth. Truth has definitely been replaced with expediency.

In arrogating to itself the role of Providence, the state deals with truth as if it were but the result of a positive, authoritative decision. That it does so without any pretension to divine capacities makes the dethronement of truth still more obvious. The question of truth is "devalued" to such an extent that no explanation seems needed for the defense of the validity of contradictory statements. The fact that they are uttered by the state is enough.

Indifference toward the question of the truth of a thing is obviously one of the worst symptoms of the perversion and desubstantialization of the human mind. It is, of course, impossible to eliminate truth completely. In raising the question whether a thing is in agreement with the proletarian mentality, one implies that the answer to this question must be either true or false. Nevertheless, the danger of attempting to replace truth with other measures, and the disrespect for the ultimate dignity of truth, cannot be denounced strongly enough.

The role of truth in human life is so predominant and decisive, the interest in the question of whether a thing is true or not is so indispensable in all the domains of human life, ranging from the most humble everyday affairs to the highest spiritual spheres, that the dethronement of truth entails the decomposition of man's very life. Disrespect for truth, when not merely a theoretical thesis, but a lived attitude, patently destroys all morality, even all reasonability and all community life. All objective norms are dissolved by this attitude of indifference toward truth; so also is the possibility of resolving any discussion or controversy objectively; peace among individuals or nations and all trust in other persons are impossible as well. The very basis of a really human life is subverted. There exists an intimate link between the dethronement of truth and terrorism. As soon as man no longer refers to truth as the ultimate judge in all spheres of life, brutal force necessarily replaces right, oppression and mechanical, suggestive influence supersedes conviction, fear supplants trust. Indeed, to dethrone truth means to sever the human person from the very basis of his spiritual existence; it is the most radical, practical atheism and thus it is deeply linked with the depersonalization of man, the anti-personalism that is the characteristic feature of Communism and of all the different types of totalitarianism. An abyss separates this decomposition of human life and of the human person from the attitude expressed in the words of St. Augustine: "O Truth, Truth, how inwardly did the very marrow of my soul pant for You . . ."[1]

Although the dethronement of truth manifests itself in the most drastic and radical way in Nazism and Bolshevism, unfortunately many symptoms of this

1. *The Confessions of Saint Augustine*, trans. F. J. Sheed (New York: Sheed & Ward, 1942), bk. 3, chap. 6, p. 47.

spiritual disease are also to be found in democratic countries.

In discussions we sometimes hear the following argument: "Why should your opinion be more valid than mine? We are equal and have the same rights. It is to pretend that your opinion is preferable." This attitude is extremely significant because it reveals the complete absence of the notion of truth, the tacit elimination of truth as the norm for the value of an opinion.

In ignoring the fact that the very essence of every opinion involves a thesis that affirms or denies some fact, such people deal with opinions as if they were mere attitudes of a subject, such as a subjective mood. The immanent theme of every opinion is truth; the only thing that matters here is whether or not it is in conformity with reality. The question of who proffers an opinion, on the contrary, has as such no importance whatever for its validity. We must realize that this argument should not be interpreted as if it meant: Your opinion has no greater chance than mine to hit upon the truth. Such an argument would not ignore truth or tacitly eliminate it. It would, on the contrary, presuppose the existence of objective truth if only by denying that our adversary has a greater capacity for finding truth. Patently, this argument could have meaning only if our opponent, in proffering an opinion, claimed its acceptance because he proffered it; or, in other words, because his authority should guarantee the truth of his opinion. Without raising here the question whether or not such a claim can be justified, there is no doubt that the equality of the intellectual capacity to grasp truth cannot be correctly inferred from the ontological equality of men or from the equality of their rights as men.

Yet, this argument is generally meant not as a refutation of an opponent's pretension to a greater competence to find truth but as a plea for the equal value or validity of both opinions. Thus it simply ignores the fact that the validity or value of an opinion depends exclusively upon its conformity to reality; that is, it no longer questions whether a statement is true or false. This argument deals with an opinion as if value depended exclusively on the person uttering it. Therefore, this modern type of man does not examine the arguments of the adversary; he is not interested in the correctness of his conclusions, the evidence of his premises, but in completely turning away from the fact that the opinion confirms or denies, he only proclaims: "My opinion is as good as yours because we are all equal." Whereas in the totalitarian systems the true function of a proposition—namely, that of stating truth—has been replaced by the merely instrumental character of being a weapon destined to create a certain effect in the mind and soul of the public, a means of propaganda, in the democratic countries there is a trend to regard an opinion as merely an expression of the mind of an individual. In both cases the essential function of any proposition and opinion that purport to conform with being is ignored and eliminated.

The argument, "My opinion is as good as yours," does not imply the tacit presupposition, "We are both unable to find truth, or at least we cannot know whether we are able to do so, and thus both our opinions are wrong or doubtful." Rather, it implies that both opinions are equally good, valid, though contrarily opposed to each other. And this brings us to another slogan disclosing the dethronement of truth. It is the often repeated "It is true for me, but it may not be true for you." The truth of a proposition is essentially objective; a truth that as such would be valid for one person only is a contradiction in terms. A proposition is true or false, but it can never be true for one person and false for another. The statement that a certain action is morally good may be true or false; but if it is true, it can never be false for any other person. The suffix "for," implying a relation to an individual, is essentially excluded in truth.

Even if the content of a proposition refers to an individual only, it is incorrect to say that it is only "true for him." If Paul says, "I arrived Friday in Pennsylvania Station in New York," the truth of the proposition implies no relation to a single person, and if it is true, it is true for everyone. The fact that only Paul, and not Harry, arrived Friday in Penn Station in no way reduces the truth of Paul's arrival to something valid only for him. The arrival applies only to Paul and not to Harry, but the fact that Paul arrived is a reality, and thus the truth of the statement "Paul arrived" is in no way relative to him. If a man claimed that "oranges are unhealthful" because he is allergic to them, his thesis would be false and not "true for him." On the contrary, "Oranges are unhealthful for me" would be a true statement: not only true for him, but true in itself.

Summarizing, we can say: A proposition, an opinion, a thesis, can never be true for one person; if it is in conformity with reality, it is true as such, and excludes any "for."

When dealing with a relation to a person, the "for" has to be in the content of the proposition, as a part of the affirmed reality, such as, for instance, "Oranges are unhealthful for Paul," or "This work is too much for Peter." If, on the contrary, someone omitted to mention the relation to himself, or to any other person, in the context of the affirmed state of facts, and said, "Oranges are unhealthful," only because he is allergic to them, his statement would be definitely false and in no way true "for him."

Certainly a person can say: "It seems to me to be true." But in saying so he in no way refers to a truth that is valid only for him. In saying, "It seems to me to be true," he wants either to state that according to his conviction it is true, or that its truth is not yet ascertained. When the stress is placed on the "seems" and not on the "to me," a restriction is imposed on our affirmation. Instead of saying that it is so, we say that it only seems to be so. The "seems" necessarily implies a relation to someone, that is, to the mind of a person. But obviously the restriction of my knowledge or conviction concerning the truth of a proposition that the "seems to me" expresses does not imply its being "true for me." The fact that it is not absolutely certain whether something is true or not affects in no way the character of truth as such. If it is true, it is not only true for me but true in itself. Nevertheless, for the moment I am able to say only, "It seems to me to be true," which is equivalent to "It is probably true."

If the stress is placed on the "to me," if, for instance, someone opposed the opinion of another by saying, "To me, this does not seem to be true," the notion of truth in its integrity is equally presupposed. This statement is equivalent to the proposition, "I believe that this is true." Of course the subject is necessarily involved, as soon as the question of considering a thing true or false is at stake. It is always a person who considers a thing to be true or false; the truth attributed to a statement by one person but not by another, however, is never a truth for someone. The relativity implied in the statement, "It seems to be true to me," is in reality nothing but the expression of the fact that I hold something true or false. Certainly I hold it true or false, but by the truth or falseness that I ascribe to a thing I mean a truth or falseness in itself. If a proposition does not correspond to reality, it is false, independently of whether or not it is held by one person or by many. We can thus clearly see that the statement, "It seems to be true to me," differs essentially from the statement, "This is true for me." The first is a correct expression of a conviction concerning the truth of a proposition; the second is a nonsensical *contradictio in adjectu*. The first in no way dethrones or desubstantializes truth; the second is a typical symptom of impairment of the notion of truth, a complete indifference toward the question of whether a thing is true or not.

Thus the slogan, "This is true for me," reveals a radical disinterest in the question of truth, a complete misunderstanding of the nature of truth, a dethronement of truth as the judge of any thesis, opinion, or theory.

There are still other symptoms of the dethronement of truth. Sometimes it would seem that for many persons the notion of progress assumes a function somewhat analogous to that of the Nordic race in Nazism and of the proletarian mentality in Communism.

For these people, the two alternatives, progressive and reactionary, have replaced the alternatives good and evil. Interest in the progressiveness of a thing has absorbed the interest in the question of its truth. The meaning of the term "progressive" is nearly as vague, void, and accidental as the meaning of the "feeling of the Nordic race" or of "the proletarian mentality."

The fact that something corresponds to the mentality of our epoch is no more decisive for its truth or value than the fact that it corresponds to the mentality of former times. The concept of progress certainly *does* sometimes imply the notion of improvement, as when we speak of moral progress or progress in knowledge, recovering health, and so on. But we also speak of the progress of an illness, of a decomposition, or of an enmity. Progress as such signifies only a more developed stage of an evolution, an intensification, without indicating whether it is a good or an evil that is developing.

To make of progressiveness the source of a consciousness of superiority, and the ultimate measure for the acceptance or rejection of a thing, is thus a further symptom of the dethronement of truth. Making a fetish of swimming with the stream of the present epoch, of keeping up to date, is bound up with a subjectivism that replaces the conformity of a theory, a thesis, or a proposition to reality, by a conformity to the "spirit" of a certain epoch. The "objectivity" a theory possesses because it comes to the person from without as an interpersonal reality, instead of being only his opinion or originating in his mind, is confused with the true objectivity resulting from conformity with being.

The historical reality possessed by ideas "in the air" replaces the authentic metaphysical reality of a thing, as well as the objective validity and truth of these ideas. The intoxication experienced in swimming with the stream of a certain epoch, in being supported by public opinion, in sharing in a new, unheard-of evolution, has replaced the sober and noble interest in truth, the respect for truth as the ultimate judge of every theory, every opinion and thesis.

Finally, a characteristic symptom of the dethronement of truth is the reasoning with which vicious ideologies and vapid theories are often refuted. Instead of proving the falsehood of materialism, racism, or collectivism, certain people will often offer the following argument as being the most conclusive: "These ideologies are not in conformity with the tradition of our country." In the Swiss press you may find, "Nazism and Communism are not in conformity with the Swiss tradition." In France, "It is against the genius of France"; in the United States, "It is incompatible with the American way of life."

Is it not alarming that even when we face these visions of hell, these false ideologies, we can trace the dethronement of truth in the very mouth of the defenders of the dignity of the person and of freedom? A deep intellectual insecurity betrays itself here: a feeling of being more sheltered and standing on firmer ground when appealing to such a completely contingent factor as a national "way of life," than when appealing to truth and objective values.

Certainly it is not their incompatibility with a national tradition that makes these systems of government and their philosophy detestable to many people who argue this way. Their horror may be a sound response to the objective disvalue of these systems and to the falsehood of their philosophy. What is so appalling is the fact that as soon as they want to utter the most decisive and stringent argument, the most "objective" one, they have recourse to an appeal that, as such, in no way proves the value or disvalue of a political system, or the truth or falsehood of its philosophy. The dethronement of truth here assumes less the character of disrespect for truth, of a radical ignoring of the question of truth, than the character of distrust toward the question of truth, of an elimination of this question. Any recourse to truth is treated as ineffectual. On the one hand, because of a basic intellectual insecurity men no longer dare to appeal to truth; on the other, they believe that the use of a completely subjective measure is a more powerful and conclusive, a sounder weapon against these errors.

If these arguments were uttered with respect to things having the character of a mere expression of national individuality, such as certain customs or cultural habits, they could be correct and certainly would in no way be alarming. Concerning, for instance, differences between forms of government, such as between monarchy and republic (which according to the doctrine of the Holy Church are equally good), such an argument would be absolutely correct. Monarchy, corresponding as it does to the tradition and way of life of England, is the right form of government for the English people; whereas monarchy would not agree with the traditions and way of life of Switzerland or the United States, and would thus be out of place there. But as soon as differences that imply either questions or ideologies are at stake, such reasoning clearly manifests the dethronement of truth.

In the face of these alarming symptoms, the question arises: What are the factors that have led to this spiritual disease? What are its causes?

The most obvious causes of the dethronement of truth are various forms of relativism, ranging from moderate subjectivism down to outright skepticism, which, with increasing rhythm, have become the "official" philosophy taught and professed in secular universities. Today it seems as if there were but one point in which the various non-Catholic philosophical theories agree, that is, the denial of the possibility of attaining objective truth. Certainly an abyss still lies between this theoretical denial of objective truth and the really accomplished and lived indifference toward it. As it happens, in his direct contact with being, man is protected for a certain length of time from accepting the assorted absurdities he may profess in his theoretical analyses.

In general, we may observe that the voice of being is so convincing that in the lived, immediate contact with it man forgets the different misconstructions he creates in reflecting theoretically upon it. Fortunately, man is not so consistent that his direct approach to being is immediately affected by his theories. Convincing and evident data, and not his absurd theories, remain the basis of his responses. When, for example, Nietzsche saw an icy road one winter, he wept out of compassion for the poor children who might fall on it, notwithstanding the fact that in his theoretical statement he declared compassion to be nothing but a symptom of deplorable weakness and of a decadence of vitality. Yet he experienced his immediate response not as a deplorable weakness but as something objectively justified. In their struggle against capitalism, the Marxists appealed to justice and to the rights of men, although theoretically they professed a materialism that left a place neither for ethical, absolute values nor for the rights of men. For, patently, a being that is not a person but merely a higher, more developed kind of matter can have no rights whatsoever.

Moreover, in life the direct approach to being remains for a certain period protected from the perversions of the intellectual sphere. We see, for instance, that from the Renaissance until the beginning of the nineteenth century art and culture were still rooted in the Christian heritage, notwithstanding the progressive spiritual secularization in the theoretical sphere that took place during this epoch. But this "protection," which was due to a fortunate inconsistency, does not last indefinitely. Whenever man becomes lost in errors, God gives him a certain period of respite. While consuming the paternal heritage, the prodigal son could live on it for a certain time. But after a little while, the heritage is exhausted. Analogously, after a certain time, errors in the theoretical sphere begin to affect man's immediate approach to being and will corrode and pervert his spontaneous attitudes.

This is what actually happens with respect to truth. The century-old propagation of relativism and subjectivism, although inconsistently implying a tacit respect for truth, affected finally the direct approach to being, and created the attitude of indifference and disrespect for truth in life itself. In the long run, man does not remain inconsistent: what is professed in theory necessarily becomes at a certain moment an informing factor of man's lived attitude. Thus the responsibility of all subjectivists and relativists for the dethronement of truth must be fully acknowledged, although, due to their inconsistency, they appealed to truth in practice.

It is not, however, exclusively thematic relativism—that is, the attack on objective truth—that is at the basis of the dethronement of truth. In Kant's gigantic system we find a complete reversal of the process and nature of knowledge. According to Kant, knowledge is understood no longer as a grasping of a being such as it is objectively—a spiritual possession of it, or an intentional participation in being—but as a process of constructing the object of our knowledge. Indeed, in this deformation of the notion of knowledge—a deformation equivalent to a denial of the very nature of knowledge—Kant is as inconsistent as any skeptic or relativist is bound to be. While claiming that in reality knowledge consists in the construction of an object, he clearly says not that he offers us a construction of knowledge, but that he has discovered the real, authentic nature of knowledge. His knowledge of the nature of knowledge is introduced as knowledge in the classical sense of that term. Clearly, Kant is doomed to inconsistency, as is any skeptic, because in trying to deny such ultimate data as being, truth, or knowledge, he necessarily presupposes them in the same breath.

Yet, having banished the knowledge of any objective, metaphysical reality, Kant introduced the dangerous notion of the *postulate* and thereby replaced truth with indispensability. Certain fundamental metaphysical facts now became no longer accepted because of their truth, that is, their reality, but merely because of their indispensability for ethics. The shift in the direction of the postulate, or of the substitution of an indispensable presupposition for truth, manifested itself already in the *Critique of Pure Reason*. The great aim of Kant's construction was to save mathematics and science from Hume's skepticism, or, as it can be said, to prove the possibility of synthetic judgments *a priori* in mathematics and in the sciences. Thus his entire way of proceeding has somehow an apologetic character. Instead of the pure thirst for truth and the genuine "wondering" of Plato and Aristotle, instead of the undistorted exploration of being as such, the most fundamental metaphysical and epistemological facts are approached under the viewpoint of a defense of such a relatively contingent and secondary object as science. Whereas Plato discovered in *Meno* the existence of an absolute objective truth independent of experience in the sense of observation and induction,[2] Kant was concerned with the hypothesis destined to save the possibility

2. Cf. Dietrich von Hildebrand, *Der Sinn Philosophischen Fragens und Erkennens* (Bonn: Peter Hanstein, 1950).

of synthetic judgments *a priori*, and he ended by sacrificing the notion of objective truth on the altar of science. He sacrificed objective truth for the sake of *a priori* judgment. Great and profound as the transcendental deduction is as a method, as an analysis of concrete experience by delving always deeper into all its metaphysical presuppositions, it is a typical case of the surgeon who declares that an operation was carried out very successfully—but unfortunately the patient died. Obviously if we abandon both the notion of knowledge as a grasping of being such as it is objectively and the notion of truth that is not merely relative to the human mind, the possibility of synthetic judgments *a priori* no longer matters.

Freedom of the will, the immortality of the soul, and even the existence of God were no longer to be proved as real facts and professed as truths, but were now merely assumed because one could not do without them. The substitution of practical indispensability for truth is a perversion of the greatest consequence. The most important facts upon which everything else depends are no longer approached from the point of view of truth, but merely from the point of view of their indispensability for ethics. Here the question of truth is even expressly suspended. Here we encounter a complete reversal of the true hierarchy of being. What is true is no longer the basis of our attitudes because it is true; instead, we accept a fact arbitrarily as if it were true, because we need it as basis for our moral life.

Some important distinctions must be made here. The notion of the postulate must not be mistaken for necessary presuppositions that we are entitled to infer from certain real data. It is in the name of objective truth that we infer, for example, the existence of a *primary cause*, from the existence of contingent beings. The existence of a contingent being guarantees our knowledge of the existence of an absolute being. This conclusion is absolutely correct. It is rooted in genuine interest in reality and is based on a valid, classical procedure leading to the attainment of knowledge.

The postulate, on the contrary, does not claim to be accessible by the process of inferring a cause from its effects. Rather, it must be presumed in order to safeguard a thing that for practical reasons (in the broader sense of the term) we cannot afford to sacrifice. The postulate shows the same lofty suspension in the air as does the categorical imperative; just as important and fundamental as is Kant's insight into the categorical character of moral obligation, as unsatisfactory is his ignoring of the value from which this categorical imperative issues. He deprives the categorical imperative of its ontological basis and even sees in this privation the condition of its objective validity. There is no reason that would guarantee the existence of a postulate. It involves, on the contrary, the elimination of the question of truth and the replacement of truth by practical indispensability. Without asking whether or not something is so in reality, we have to accept it for the sake of its indispensable role in our life.

The postulate must also be distinguished from the hypothesis. The hypothesis, though a construction offered as a possible explanation of a phenomenon and not the necessary result of an inference, is nevertheless an attempt in the direction of finding a truth, and with the demonstration of its plausibility it is definitely placed under the aegis of truth. It appeals to our "critical" reason and not to our "practical" reason.

Third, we must distinguish between the indispensability of the postulate and the classical character of a truth manifesting itself through its fundamental congeniality with the totality of the cosmos. We mentioned above that man in his direct contact with being often contradicts his own theories. But we are not thinking of the fact that in our weakness we often do not act in conformity with the principles our reason accepts as true. We mean that in confronting being an immediate, lived contact, reality gives the lie to many absurd theories that are the result of abstract constructions and are obtained by deducing them by means of doubtful syllogisms, from vague premises, instead of by listening to reality. Someone, for example, may theoretically deny the existence of objective moral good and evil, but as soon as he is confronted with a noble moral action or a mean, wicked attitude, forgetting his artificial theory, he will grasp the elementary reality of objective moral values.

This correction of abstract, artificial theories by the undistorted voice of reality, the voice of reality that has not been silenced by prejudices, takes place in the frame of knowledge and appeals to truth instead of to practical indispensability. Thus we are not merely *postulating* the objective reality of moral values when, in arguing against the moral relativist, we proffer as argument the fact that he admits objective moral values in his life—at least in his response of indignation or admiration. We are by no means suspending the question of truth by arguing so. We do not rely on the mere statement: "You have to give up your theory because it does not work. You must, in any case, suppose objective moral values, or you will not get far." No, we claim, on the contrary, that in the naïve and immediate contact with being the relativist grasps intuitively the reality of the very thing he tries to deny on the theoretical plane. We claim that his theory is the result not of a real insight but of the artificial combination of prejudices, unproved, tacit presuppositions, sophistical pseudo-arguments; and that it is even dictated by many motives that are extraneous to the sphere of reason, being an intrusion of pride and concupiscence. Conversely, the conviction informing his immediate contact with being is the result of a real perception; it is the result of the convincing power of reality, which reveals itself independently of all prejudices, and though the knowledge in question is not a critical and systematic one, it gives evidence of the objective existence of moral values, and is genuine and valid knowledge.

Various ways exist in which a metaphysical reality may reveal itself to our mind, and it would be ridiculous to claim that only the way that can be deduced *more geometrico* addresses itself to our intellect. The sphere of our intelligence reaches farther than that of mathematical deduction. To appeal to an experience of a thing immediately given[3] without being able to prove it with arguments does not mean to suspend the question of truth and to substitute something else for it. The question of truth surpasses by far the range even of that which can be grasped by human intelligence. We shall see later on that a false, fossilized rationalism has its share of responsibility in the dethronement of truth, although in a more indirect way. But the postulate definitely involves the suspension of the question of truth and its displacement by practical indispensability. By taking refuge in the notion of the postulate, we accept a metaphysical truth not because it manifests itself in its intrinsic truth and classical character; rather, we behave only *as if* it were so, because we *cannot manage without it*.

The line that leads from the postulate to Vaihinger's "as-if philosophy" and to pragmatism is obvious. And it is not difficult to see that the attitude

3. Cf. Dietrich von Hildebrand, *Ethics* (Steubenville: Hildebrand Press, 2020), 1–20.

itself in these theories has, in gaining more and more currency, contributed largely to the dethronement of truth.

A third cause of this dethronement is historicism. The relativism that results from seeing every philosophy and theory as a mere historical phenomenon tacitly eliminates truth as the norm and fixes our attention on the significance of an idea as an expression of a certain epoch. This attitude is brilliantly described by C. S. Lewis:

> The Historical Point of View, put briefly, means that when a learned man is presented with any statement in an ancient author, the one question he never asks is whether it is true. He asks who influenced the ancient writer, and how far the statement is consistent with what he said in other books, and what phase in the writer's development, or in the general history of thought, it illustrates, and how it affected later writers, and how often it has been misunderstood (specially by the learned man's own colleagues) and what the general course of criticism on it has been for the last ten years, and what is the "present state

> of the question." To regard the ancient writer as a possible source of knowledge—to anticipate that what he said could possibly modify your thoughts or your behavior—this would be rejected as unutterably simpleminded.[4]

The poison of historicism is specifically dangerous for two reasons. First, historicism is a perversion of valuable and important truths. Second, it is not directly concerned with the denial of objective truth, but in focusing itself exclusively on the historical aspect it tacitly eliminates the question of truth. In stating that historicism is a perversion or an abuse of valuable insights we are thinking of the undoubtedly true fact that in the exploration of philosophical truths there exists a historical rhythm; for the full philosophical comprehension of fundamental facts requires a certain historical moment—its hour in history, requires, moreover, that an evolution of ideas has prepared this possibility, and so on. It is not by accident that Aristotle's discovery of the four causes was preceded by the Presocratics, by Socrates, and by Plato. Hegel's theory of a development

4. *The Screwtape Letters* (New York: Macmillan Inc., 1944), 139–40.

of the objective *logos* in history has undoubtedly hit upon something true, questionable though his entire conception may be. But interesting and important as the historical aspect of a philosophical theory may be, it is secondary in comparison with the question whether the insight is true or not, whether the theory is in conformity with being or not, and to what extent it is so.

Historicism does not content itself with examining the role of the rhythm of history in the exploration of truth, nor with the limitations due to certain historical intellectual situations, but it reduces the entire significance of a religious, metaphysical, or ethical conception to its historical function. When we, for instance, hear praise of St. Augustine, or of St. Anselm, we expect to find some concordance between the position of the author and one of these saints; but we expect it in vain. Enthusiastic and apparently sympathetic as the appreciation of these philosophers may be, any position toward the truth or falsehood of their ideas is avoided. We find it stated only how great they were for their time, how well they expressed their time. Intelligence and spiritual stature have become here the decisive norm, and no longer the truth or falsehood of their insights.

Skepticism and positivism, which deny objective truth, are comparatively more concerned with truth. Rebellion and enmity against objective truth at least regard the question of truth more seriously than does historicism. Historicism treats the question whether a theory is true or not as of no interest, or even as if it were a naïve and crude approach to an opinion, a philosophical system, or an ideology.

Its approach to religion is specifically typical of historicism. Whereas atheists still take seriously the question of God's existence, the historicist seems not even to understand the immanent pretension of religion, but looks at it merely as an interesting cultural and historical phenomenon. He treats the different religions with equal sympathy and expounds their doctrines with apparent respect and benevolent understanding. He views them apparently not "from without," but from within, but this "from within" means an immanentism that has once and for all tacitly eliminated the great decisive question whether this religion is true or not. In reality this seemingly sympathetic approach is the ultimate climax of a distorted view from without, because it deprives religion of its innermost meaning, which is truth, divinely revealed absolute truth, which the

Credo affirms and for which martyrs have shed their blood. In cutting off faith from truth—its objective correlate—and in making of it an interesting expression of the human mind, historicism desubstantializes religion to a greater extent than the man who denied God the name of objective truth.

A typical fruit of historicism is the position toward the Holy Church taken in the *Action Française*, and especially the writings of Charles Maurras. Maurras praises the Church for its cultural and political function, the value that it embodies in history, and above all for its "latinity." He eulogizes the Church because it is so wonderfully pagan. Is this favorable judgment of the Church not a greater offense and misunderstanding than a furious attack on the part of Protestants, who reproach her for being not faithful enough to Christ? Unthinking and shocking as it is, the Protestant reproach takes more seriously than did Charles Maurras the claim of the Church to teach divine truth and the words of Christ.

Finally, the predominance of a psychological approach and the triumphant march of psychoanalysis also had their share in preparing the dethronement of truth. The interest in psychological reasons—why a person utters an opinion, affirms a thesis, holds a position toward a theory—has replaced more and more the interest in the question of the truth of this opinion, this thesis or theory. Justified as this approach may be in many cases, indispensable as it is to examine this question in order to judge a person and decide how to deal with him, as soon as it supplants the question of the truth of the opinion, a disastrous perversion takes place.

When upon hearing a theory concerning metaphysical problems one asks only what psychological motives may be behind it, instead of examining whether or not this theory is in conformity with reality, his approach is in many respects perverted; he should be primarily interested in the *truth* of this theory. A sound approach is primarily concerned with the content of a thesis, with its claim to being true. There must be some special reason to justify turning away from the object and focusing on the soul of the person who utters a theory. One reason can be that we are professional psychologists. But even in this case, the question whether an opinion is false or true has an eminent importance for our psychological analysis. If the theory is true, special psychological motives are not necessarily required in order to explain why a person professes this theory. On the contrary, man's normal motivation for holding an opinion is the compelling force of the reality his intellect grasps. It would certainly be bad psychology to eliminate fom the beginning the possibility that a person's motivation for holding a thesis is simply the fact that reality has disclosed to him that it is so. As long as a theory is true, or insofar as it is true, there is normally no other motivation at stake than the truth, and all that we have to analyze in the mind of the person holding the theory is the nature of his knowledge, conviction, and judgment. This analysis, however, concerns only the explanation of how a person can acquire knowledge and objectivate it in a thesis; but the reason for holding an opinion remains the truth of this theory or the existence of this fact. In errors we may look for "psychological" reasons, but as long as a true statement is in question, we have no reason to look for subjective motives.

Thus we have to state that even a psychologist must inquire whether a theory, a statement, or a judgment is true or not before he can examine the psychological condition of the one uttering it, because the question of its truth has a paramount importance even for deciding whether a psychological problem is involved or not.

Of course, there can also be extraordinary cases in which we have to look for psychological reasons, though the judgment or the thesis is true. A person may be either hysterical or cut off by his self-centeredness from all genuine contact with being and the world surrounding him. In this case, even if he states the truth, we do not believe that his statement is the genuine result of the dictates of being; though the content of his judgment is true, we doubt that a real interest in truth is at the basis of his judgment. On the other hand, he may be dishonest, and then we mistrust him to such an extent that *what* he is saying no longer matters, but exclusively *why* he is saying it. We presume in such a case that this man's statement is merely a means for attaining a practical purpose. This psychological approach is the only reasonable one when we have to deal with persons who have completely dethroned truth, such as, for example, Hitler or Stalin. But the fact that, when dealing with an opinion or a statement, in case of moral perversion or mental abnormality, the only thing to do is to turn to a psychological research clearly reveals that such an approach is inadequate under normal conditions. The factors that are responsible for an illness and that explain its origins cannot be present in the healthy person. If the statement is false, it may be necessary to examine whether psychological reasons answer for the error, but, as mentioned above, we must first ascertain whether it is true or false. Moreover, the psychological explanation of the error does not dispense us from a rational refutation of it. In order to help the person who, for moral reasons, cleaves to a wrong theory or even merely acts as though he did, we, for our part, must start from the firm ground of objective truth. Only if we ourselves start from the basis of that which is objectively true shall we be able to help other persons to overcome the moral and psychological obstacles barring them from truth.

Above all, we must realize that the real nature and validity of the higher acts of the person can be understood only by including their object in our analysis. It is the very nature of conviction to be convinced that something is so; of the nature of joy, to be joyful about something. As long as we ignore the object to which the conviction or joy is responding, its nature and its value, an evaluation of the act is impossible.

It is a basic error to regard personal acts as though they could be understood independently of their intentional character; a basic error to approach this ambient as though it were composed of mere states and accessible to an immanent and causal analysis, undermining the interest in the truth of an opinion or judgment and substituting for the question, "What is he stating?" the question, "Why is he stating it?"

Here one may rightly ask: If relativism, pragmatism, historicism, and psychologism have brought about the dethronement of truth, what is the cause of all these different "isms" and, especially, of the fact that they did not remain in the theoretical realm but infected and corroded the naïve, lived approach to being?

The present educational system has its responsibility in the corrosion of the masses' naïve approach to being. In our epoch, and especially in the United States, the ideal that everybody should be instructed, that everybody should have an intellectual education, is widespread. The conviction that everything can be learned if properly taught, that a high good would be unjustly withheld from a person if he did not receive his share of the modern treasure of knowledge, is at the basis of this ideal. Without discussing the truth of these two presuppositions, we can easily see that the new situation concerning the instruction of the masses opens the door for spreading pseudo-philosophies among the public. Through the new educational ideal, the decoction of all these destructive "isms" is poured into the minds of young people and respectfully accepted by them. To this, let us still add the perpetual "massage" of our minds by movies, newspapers, magazines, and radio, and we can understand why the dethronement of truth today remains no longer the province of certain professors but has successfully infected the immediate approach to being of the average man.[5]

Nevertheless, it is true that we must dig still deeper in order to reach the ultimate roots of the dethronement of truth. Indeed, we do not claim that we are able to unveil the origin of a perversion of the mind such as this, because ultimately it is as mysterious as the origin of evil itself. But the one element behind those theoretical denials or eliminations of truth, as well as behind the entire attitude manifesting itself in these theories, is accessible to our analysis. It is the apostasy from God, the rebellion

5. Cf. *The New Tower of Babel* 14ff.

of man against the Father of all truth, the refusal to accept the condition of a creature and the glorious vocation of being an image of God. In trying to shake off the *religio*—that is, the fundamental of dependence upon God, the obligation toward God in which we are embedded, the ordination toward God—we necessarily become victims of falsehood and corrode our basic relation to truth. The attitude of *non serviam* (I will not serve), the desire to follow the temptation of *eritis sicut dii* (you will be like gods), the rebellion against God, is the ultimate root of the dethronement of truth.

The problem of showing how to overcome the dethronement of truth is by far more difficult than that of tracing its sources. We shall restrict ourselves in our analysis to inquiring how we should fight against it.

First, the classic refutation of all brands of skepticism and relativism should time and again be emphasized. As far as the influence of relativism and positivism is concerned, we have to eradicate it with philosophical arguments. We should not fear to appear old-fashioned, antiquated, or even banal in repeating what loses neither its power nor its profundity by having often been stated. The fact that the modern denial of objective truth has more the character of an unchallengeable presupposition than that of a positive thesis—as in skepticism—must not divert our attention and lead us to a suspension of this question while we deal with philosophy. It is a kind of snobbishness that hinders many thinkers from restating again and again the strict refutation of all forms of skepticism. They shun the appearance of being undifferentiated, primitive, and without any sense for the problems of our epoch. Certainly the unmasking of the intrinsic contradiction and inconsistency of any and every denial of objective truth should not be proffered as a merely schematic and bloodless formula. To repeat it again and again does not mean to repeat a stereotyped formula; on the contrary, its every repetition contains a full insight that, in all its inexhaustible power, unmasks the empty and nonsensical character of every radical skepticism. As Goethe rightly said: "Error finds ceaseless repetition in deed, for which reason one must never tire of repeating the truth in words."[6]

6. "Maxims and Reflections," 331 (1826), in *Goethe, Wisdom and Experience*, ed. Ludwig Curtius, trans. H. J. Weigand (New York: Routledge & Kegan Paul LTD, 1949), 126.

We must realize that the inconsistency of radical relativism is such that a philosopher who even tacitly presupposes the denial of objective truth has objectively condemned his entire philosophy. Even more, every scientist who denies the possibility of attaining objective truth utters senseless words, mere babbling.

We must insist on the ridiculous inconsistency of all those who profess a denial of objective truth and simultaneously arrogate objective truth to their theory. Nothing can be more fatal to a theory than to deny in its content what it necessarily presupposes in the very act of affirming. We must not cease unmasking the inevitable, flagrant contradiction that is necessarily involved in every attempt to deny objective truth and the possibility of its knowledge. More and more contradictions are heaped upon this immanent contradiction between the content of an affirmation and the implicit formal claim of every affirmation as such. When offering arguments or even writing whole books to prove the thesis that absolute truth does not exist, these relativists presuppose various facts as incontrovertible: first, the premises from which they start arguing; second, the validity of the principles of logic on which their conclusions are based. As soon as they suspend the validity of either one of the above-mentioned presuppositions, their arguments or their theses lose all power and collapse completely.

Likewise, we must stress again and again that Kant's dissolution of the authentic meaning of knowledge as the grasping of a being such as it is objectively (or, to use the traditional term, as the intentional partaking of the very nature of a being) by replacing it with the notion of the construction of the object, implies an immanent contradiction. Thereby Kant claims to grasp the nature of knowledge such as it is, and to offer not merely a subjective construction of what knowledge is. The fact that he considers his thesis as a fundamental discovery, as a "Copernican turning," clearly testifies to this claim. Thus we encounter here an immanent contradiction in the interpretation of knowledge, analogical to the one that is part and parcel of any relativism with respect to objective truth. In *claiming* to reveal to us the real nature of knowledge, Kant presupposes the notion of knowledge that he denies in the content of his thesis.

Again, analogically, this contradiction is clearly to be found in pragmatism. When pragmatism claims that truth means nothing but usefulness and that a proposition is true when it is a useful basis for our practical tasks, truth in its authentic meaning is implicitly presupposed. The pragmatist wants to prove that truth is really nothing else than usefulness and claims that this statement at least is true and not only useful. If he were to deny this, the meaning of his thesis would collapse completely. Likewise, he refers to truth in its authentic sense in all his premises and conclusions. In proffering arguments for his thesis, the pragmatist tacitly presupposes his premises to correspond to real facts, and presupposes his conclusions the truth of logical principles. Even the statement that a concrete idea is useful presupposes truth; it involves the claim that the idea is truly useful. All attempts to deny objective truth and to change its meaning or the meaning of knowledge necessarily involve an immanent contradiction, because truth and knowledge are elementary, ultimate, evident data presupposed in any affirmation and thesis. He who tries to deny these ultimate data behaves like a man who wants to jump behind himself.

If we want to fight the dethronement of truth, we must above all abandon a predominantly defensive attitude in the philosophical arena. For centuries the philosophical energy of many scholastic philosophers has been absorbed by a distorted defense of Thomism. The question whether some philosophical thesis proffered by a non-Catholic or by a Catholic philosopher is true or not seems to have become equivalent to the question whether it can be found directly or indirectly in Thomism.

Instead of trying and to confront it with reality, frequently one has only approached it in remaining imprisoned in a certain traditional set of concepts and often even in a traditional vocabulary; without taking the trouble of consulting reality by an immediate approach to it, one has only confronted the thesis with a Thomistic textbook, and condemned it as soon as it stated anything that had not been said in it.

An unfortunate, implicit misconception of philosophy is here at stake. Philosophy is often identified with a logically consistent system in which everything must be fitted with everything else. Though Descartes's ideal is blamed as rationalistic, an equally rationalistic notion of philosophy and process of philosophical discovery is unconsciously presupposed. It is a "logicization" of reality and its mysteries. Chevalier opposed this kind of rationalism when he said:

> We have had to wait until these past years, we have had to wait until this very war (1914) for Pascal the thinker to be given his true rank: the first. It is because the war has reminded us or has revealed to us what philosophy should truly be: not a vain dialectical game of concepts, but the answer to questions that man asks himself when facing death.[7]

Whether a Thomist or not, a true philosopher struggles to delve always deeper into the inexhaustible plenitude of being, to discover new aspects and truths; and in doing this he will be more faithful to reality than to a "system" that he has built up. We notice in the history of philosophy that great philosophers did not shrink from asserting what reality discloses to them, even though it may not fit into some theories they have built up. They do not let themselves be severed from reality by concepts they

7. *Pascal* (Paris, 1925), 7.

have formed and theses they have reached as deductions from former insights.

Sometimes the philosophical *eros*—the "wondering" and the desire to consult reality time and again—are replaced by a preoccupation with defending every detail of the Aristotelian-Thomistic system. What is legitimate and even obligatory with respect to revealed truth as formulated in the dogmas of the Church is here unconsciously applied to a philosophical system.

This attitude not only frustrates any philosophical exploration but also does injustice to the great philosophical achievement of St. Thomas. Instead of understanding that it is impossible to remain faithful to the conception of a great philosopher if we do not strive to discover for ourselves the data from which he took his point of departure, the intuition that was the starting point for his concepts, it is often believed that it suffices to give abstract definitions of concepts, and it seems satisfactory if the path leading from one concept to another is smooth and logically correct.

Sometimes these philosophers have nothing in common with the one whose disciples they claim to be beyond mere terminology. Thus, also from the point of view of doing justice to a great and venerable philosopher, we must go back to *being*, to an intellectual intuition of the reality he discovered, and we must be more anxious to remain faithful to this discovery than to his conceptualization of it and, all the more, than to his terminology.

But above all we must be more eager to find truth than to examine whether something is in agreement with the system of a philosopher, great as the philosopher may be. If a genuine appreciation of a philosopher by an historian of philosophy already requires that the philosopher's thought be confronted with reality and measured by truth, we must in a systematic exploration of reality give way *a fortiori* to the imperturbable inquiry after truth.

This true appreciation implies that we never let ourselves be barred from the immediate approach to reality by becoming prisoners of fossilized concepts, by being unable to leave a smooth, habitual track, frustrating any fertile contact with being and any enrichment, completion, and correction of the philosophical achievement of a great and venerated master. In this sense, Sciacca writes in honor of Blondel's memory:

> This magazine ... will continue to honor his memory and to participate in his thought in the only way in which one truly honors the memory of a philosopher and in which one demonstrates the vitality of his speculation: in deepening the problems of Christian philosophy with Blondel, but beyond Blondel.[8]

Some philosophers seem to confine true philosophical work to a mere elaboration of all immanent consequences of the Thomist system, a work that can be achieved by intellectual acuteness without consulting reality. Others see the main task of philosophy to lie in an integration of modern scientific and psychological results within the system—that is to say, its enlargement by elements belonging to the extra-philosophical sphere. It is clear, however, that every true philosophical work consists in an always renewed and continued exploration of being and in the confrontation of all the concepts of the school with reality. Only this can give us the possibility of appreciating fully the discovery that led to the formation of these concepts, and of enriching and

8. "Maurice Blondel," *Giornale de Metafisica* (July–August 1949): 330.

completing former results, of proceeding to new differentiations, and sometimes of eliminating artificial problems resulting only from too vague a use of certain terms.

If we gratefully accept Aristotle's distinction of the four causes and the metaphysical relations based on them, should we therefore *ab ovo* exclude the possibility that there may be still other metaphysical principles than those discovered by Aristotle? Why should we not have the right to explore being with the same unprejudiced approach and openness of intellect as did Aristotle?

> Let the foregoing suffice as our account of the views concerning the soul which have been handed on by our predecessors; let us now dismiss them and make as it were a completely fresh start, endeavoring to give a precise answer to the question, "What is soul?"[9]

Why should it be excluded *ab ovo* that an unprejudiced analysis of being could in an analogous way surpass Aristotle's conquest of the four causes, as his

9. *De anima II*, in *Basic Works of Aristotle*, trans. Richard McKeon (New York: Random House, 1941), 554.

discovery surpassed the knowledge of the Presocratics? Do we in any way do injustice to Aristotle's discovery, do we deny the truth of his distinction between the *efficient cause* and the *final cause*, if our analysis of reality compels us to admit that there exist still other causes or fundamental metaphysical relations? Is it not the worst offense to a great philosopher for us to presume that he claims to have discovered everything, seen all problems and answered them completely—a pretension that would be precisely the absolute antithesis of the Socratic statement, "I know but one thing, that I know not"?[10] What, precisely, distinguishes the true philosopher from the mere schoolmaster is the consciousness that the plenitude and depth of being surpass incomparably the range of true insights he may have gained.

True philosophy must always clearly distinguish between truths that are the result of real insight, referring to data given or accessible through strict deduction, and mere hypotheses, which can never be verified or proved themselves, but can only be judged according to their plausibility.

10. Plato, *Apology*, 20ff.

The distinction between empirical knowledge and the absolutely certain knowledge of strictly necessary, intelligible facts in Plato's *Meno* is, for instance, a classical example of a fundamental philosophical discovery, of an insight based on something evidently given. The anamnesis theory, on the contrary, is a typical hypothesis destined to explain the possibility of *a priori* knowledge, but proffering propositions and theses that cannot be verified as such, because they refer to what is accessible neither to our experience (intuitive or inductive) nor to deduction.

The distinction between a proposition referring to a sphere of reality accessible to intellectual intuition or to deduction, on the one hand, and a proposition referring to a sphere of reality inaccessible to intuition and deduction, on the other, neither denies the necessity and value of a hypothesis nor excludes the possibility that a hypothesis may be objectively in full conformity with reality. But as soon as we no longer distinguish them clearly, and deal with a hypothesis as if it were an undeniable, evident fact, we risk barring ourselves from reality. We then approach being through a network of concepts resulting from a hypothesis; and not only do we interpret every datum in the light of this hypothesis, but also we lose contact with the immediately given. We then infer how being should be from concepts that are stripped of their original content; above all, we waste our intellectual energy on artificial problems arising exclusively from the fossilization of certain concepts. Being has so many mysteries that are philosophically yet unexplored; it offers so many data of which the philosophical comprehension is still lacking, that it seems unbelievable that so much intelligence should be squandered in solving imaginary problems arising only from nonexistent alternatives, or from the extension of certain concepts into spheres of being in which they have no basis in reality.

Many terms are used in so broad a manner that the differences in meaning (which are precisely what matters) are not really grasped. Will, for instance, is used as embracing all meaningful affective responses—that is, love, admiration, esteem. What today we have in mind, however, in speaking of will is the specific response directed to something not yet real, the content of which could be circumscribed as "thou shalt be," an act that is free in the full sense of the word and that is the master of all actions. The will in this specific sense is the *exemplary cause* for every attitude we include in this term. And thus in calling love an act of will, we falsify *de facto* the very nature of love, the specific quiddity of love, which distinguishes it from all other responses. We must realize the danger resulting from using certain terms when we define them in a completely analogous sense but use them in a much more univocal sense as soon as we apply them concretely. Such is the use of the term "final." If we want to use it in a sense in which it covers every meaningful direction toward something, not only must we clearly distinguish this general term from the original meaning of *final cause*, but also we must not allow the "means-and-end" relation to remain in our mind as the hidden pattern of finality.

We must come back to a lively continuation of the magnificent process of real philosophical exploration leading from the Presocratics to Socrates, Plato, Aristotle, St. Augustine, St. Bonaventure, St. Thomas Aquinas, to a full restoration of the "wondering" before the cosmos in its inexhaustible depth.[11]

Only a philosophy that is filled with the true

11. Cf. Hildebrand, *Ethics*, 1–20.

philosophical *eros*, which reveals to us in all its rhythm the words of St. Augustine, *Quod desiderat anima fortius quam veritatem* (for what does the soul more strongly desire than the truth),[12] can do away with the discredit of reason and truth and restore full respect for truth in all domains of life. Only a philosophy that is deeply rooted in a live awareness of the plenitude of being will restore to philosophy its organic role of opening our eyes to the mysteries of being, of deepening our lived contact with being, and preparing our spirit for the infinitely superior truth of revelation, the true sense of *philosophia ancilla theologiae* (philosophy is the handmaid of theology). To the inconsistency of modern subjectivists who strive for ideals the ontological presupposition of which they deny—like the upright atheist of 1848 who thanked God every morning that He made him an atheist—there must be opposed a full consistency, that is, a lived truth, revealing in our approach to whatever practical problem that we are "rooted and founded" (Ephesians 3:17) in the fundamental natural truths, and above all, in Christ, "who is the solution of all problems." How often do we meet

12. Tract. 26 in *Joannem*, 4, 5.

Catholics who deny Christ and even fundamental natural truths as soon as they face social or political problems in the practical realm of life! To allow the light of natural and supernatural truth to penetrate fully every problem is the principal way to restore the full respect for truth as the supreme judge in all questions and as the norm of our attitudes.

The task of the reinstauration of truth implies, above all, the eradication of the moral roots that led to this disastrous attitude toward truth. In "Catholicism and Unprejudiced Knowledge"[13] we shall deal with this aspect. Here it may suffice to stress that, in order to reestablish the respect for truth and the acceptance of its character of supreme judge, any merely intellectual counteraction will not suffice. If abuses of distorted reason have led to the dethronement of truth and opened the way for the deification of all that is inferior to man and to human reason, only the suprarational light of Christ can reestablish truth in its God-given place and bring reason back to its ordainment toward truth; in other words, reestablish even reason and save it from self-destruction.

13. Cf. *The New Tower of Babel*, 132ff.

THE UNDERMINING OF TRUTH

Enamored of our present epoch, blind to all its characteristic dangers, intoxicated with everything modern, there are many Catholics who no longer ask whether something is true, or whether it is good and beautiful, or whether it has an intrinsic value: they ask only whether it is up-to-date, suitable to "modern man" and the technological age, whether it is challenging, dynamic, audacious, progressive.

Yet there is a tendency that is more refined than the subordination of truth to the fashions of our time. This is the attempt to interpret the notion of truth in a way that amounts to undermining its very content. This error is presented in an orthodox and

This text first appears as Chapter 21 in Hildebrand's *Trojan Horse in the City of God*. In the 1967 edition the chapter is titled "The Sapping of Truth."

religious guise and so is more dangerous to faith. We are referring to the distinction, gaining popularity, between "Greek" and "biblical" notions of truth.

It is a typical feature of our sociology-oriented age to present the most elementary data of human experience as deriving from the mentalities of certain nations and cultures.[1] This intellectual fashion becomes particularly absurd when applied to truth. The authentic notion of truth is in fact so fundamental and indispensable that even attempts to give it a "new" interpretation presuppose it. Truth is not a national, or cultural, or epochal property.

Truth is the conformity of a statement to reality, to the existing facts. The entire emphasis is laid on the fact that something is really thus and so. The sphere of being to which the statement refers may vary, but the test of truth remains the same. The proposition may refer to a general law, to an essential relation, or to a concrete fact. The statements "Moral values presuppose persons" and "Napoleon died at St. Helena" do not differ in quantum truth, however much the realities referred to differ.

1. Cf. Fr. Bernard Lonergan, S.J ., the address delivered at Marquette University, 12 May 1965. Similar ideas are developed by Thomas Sartory.

A true statement, whether in philosophy or empirical science, is one that possesses objective validity and is thus opposed to falsity, to the non-validity of an affirmed illusion or fiction. Moreover, the truth of a statement referring to a concrete fact—so-called historical truth—does not differ from the truth of universal statements. The source of its truth is the actual existence of the fact. To say there is a truth that has an historical stamp is therefore quite ambiguous. The reality to which the truth refers is, of course, an historical event. But the truth itself is not historical. That Napoleon died at St. Helena is true, was true fifty years ago, and will always be true. Thus, there is no "historical truth," only a truth about historical facts.

Even though truth is in the first instance predicated of the proposition, it remains completely focused on the existence of some being—whether a concrete fact or an ideal state-of-affairs. In other words, the very soul of truth is the existence of the being to which it refers. The question "Is it so, or is it not?" is equivalent to the question "Is it true, or is it not?" To see in truth something merely logical, something belonging merely to the conceptual order, is to miss its all-important existential impact.

What decides the question of whether a statement is true or not is exclusively the reality of the being in question. Thus, we must realize that truth reaches as far as being does. Truth is the echo of being. It is therefore absolutely wrong to create any antagonism between "Greek" truth, which belongs to the sphere of propositions, and a "biblical" truth, which is concerned with reality and being. The reference to being is indissolubly linked to truth, whether the being is of a metaphysical or an historical nature, whether the existence in question is a general idea or a concrete, individual fact. To every possible being there corresponds the truth of a potential statement about its existence or the nature of its existence.

There is nothing that is beyond the purview of truth, be it in the realm of our possible knowledge or outside of it, whether a mystery or something accessible to rational knowledge. Even the agnostic presupposes the existence of truth, though he declares that we cannot attain it. It should be clear that it is utterly ridiculous to interpret the most elementary fact, the most indispensable question of truth as a specialty of the Greek mind. In every question of daily life, whether of the most primitive person or the most sophisticated, truth is assumed. Whether we accuse a man of being a liar or whether we trust him, the question of truth continues to be taken for granted.

Yet it is claimed that "Greek truth" differs from "biblical truth," not only because the former is philosophical and abstract while the latter is historical but also because Greek truth is coextensive with "knowledge" (whether ethical, metaphysical, or logical) whereas biblical truth concerns the realm of faith. It is important to see that the confusion generated here results from equating two basic distinctions: that between philosophical and historical truth, and that between truths of knowledge and truths of faith. To claim that biblical truth—"faith"—refers exclusively to historical fact is most certainly incorrect. Though history indeed plays a predominant role in the Old and New Testaments, there are many fundamental facts that have no historical character and are nonetheless part of divine revelation. That Moses received the Decalogue on Mt. Sinai is an historical fact. But the content of the Decalogue can hardly be called historical. That God gave these commandments to man might be said to be something historical, but their intrinsic goodness and universal applicability is certainly not an historical fact. Christ's remark "He who calls his brother 'fool' shall deserve the fire of Gehenna" is certainly not an historical truth. And in the statement "He who believes will attain eternal life" we are again confronted with a general truth that applies to every human being. Thus, it is completely wrong to declare that the Bible, especially the New Testament, is concerned only with historical facts.

Certainly all the truths in the Bible, especially those of the New Testament, have an existential character, in the very Kierkegaardian sense of the term. They are all related to ultimate, divine reality and to the *unum necessarium* (the one thing that is necessary). But this existential character cannot be expressed by saying, as some do, that these truths have an historical coloration. This would. seem to imply—the term, of course, is ambiguous—that a truth that is historical is less absolute than non-historical truth, or that it is in some way dependent on the course of history.

There is a real distinction between knowledge and conviction, on the one hand, and divine revelation and faith, on the other. But in no sense does it concern the notion of truth. Truth is always one and the same. It consists, rather, in the enormous disparity between those things which are in principle accessible to our reason and those other things, presented in divine revelation, which in principle surpass all possible rational understanding. It follows that there will be a decisive difference between faith and conviction based on rational knowledge.

The difference between the objects of "reason" and those of "faith" is obvious. But this difference has no consequence for the notion of truth. The Holy Trinity, the beatific vision, the resurrection of the body—each either exists or does not exist, and the profession of these mysteries is either true or not. The sentence "Christ rose from the dead" does not differ in quantum truth from any other true statement—however supremely incomparable it may be as a reality.

But we must see another important distinction when we consider faith and natural conviction. It does not imply a duality in truth, but it is vital in the realm of faith. This is the distinction between "faith in" and "faith that" made by Martin Buber and Gabriel Marcel.

Without any doubt, there is a decisive difference between, on the one hand, the act of surrendering to

Christ, the response to the ineffable epiphany of God in the Sacred Humanity of Christ and, on the other hand, our accepting a mystery that Christ reveals to us. The first act—the faith in—is the fundamental religious experience. It is the response of Abraham when he felt like dust and ashes in the confrontation with the absolute person and complete otherness of God—the mysterious, infinite superiority which Rudolf Otto describes in his *The Idea of the Holy.*[2] This total, adoring giving ourselves up to the person of God is the "faith in." We find it exemplified in many places in the Gospel—in the Apostles answering the call of Christ, in the one who, when asked, "Dost thou believe?" fell down and adored Him. This act surpasses rational conviction; it is a specific surrender to a person. It occurs only in relation to a person. Even more, it must be a surrender to the Absolute Person, either to God (as in Moses), or to the self-revealed God in Christ (as in the Apostles). The "faith in" is not a theoretical response such as the belief that something exists, the object of which is a state of facts, but an all-embracing act in which

2. Rudolf Otto, *The Idea of the Holy*, 2nd ed. (New York: Oxford University Press, 1950).

the person completely surrenders mind, will, and heart to the Absolute Person. As a response to the Infinite Holiness of God, it calls for the giving up of all critical distance, all proving and testing. Yet it is simultaneously pervaded by the unshakable conviction that this response is due and that it is the very opposite of being overwhelmed simply by the dynamism of something—of being swamped and carried away by an irresistible passion, by a force experienced as stronger than ourselves. No, this "faith in" is animated by the free sanction I have described in *Christian Ethics*. It is filled with the experience of a lived confrontation with the Incarnate Truth. Such was the experience of St. Paul on the way to Damascus and of Pascal as described in his famous document, *The Memorial*. Yet in every prayer to God there is a definite actualization of the "faith in."

The "faith that" is seen in our response to all the realities revealed by Christ. We believe that there is an eternal life, that our body will really rise, that our eternal salvation depends upon our following Christ; and we believe these things because Christ has revealed them to us. This faith is a definite theoretical response; its objects are states of fact and not persons. Different as it is from any merely rational conviction (for example, of a metaphysical truth based on knowledge), "faith that" is closer to it than is "faith in"; for the theme here is truth: the sayings of Christ are believed to be true.

Now, it is clear that both "faith in" and "faith that" are involved in our Christian faith. The "faith in" is the very basis of the faith that. Objectively, our faith *in* Christ is the foundation for believing *that* what Christ has revealed is true. Moreover, "faith in" belongs to every fully religious life. There is, to be sure, the danger that many will accept religion purely as a matter of inheritance, in which case "faith that" will take precedence over "faith in," and the latter will recede well into the background. But everyone who possesses a "faith in" will always have a "faith that," as well.

The role of truth in "faith that" is obvious. It is apparent in the Credo. It would be nonsensical to claim (as Sartory and others do) that a person does not hold the content of his "faith that" to be real, authentic, and objectively valid. He must necessarily affirm that this content is true. But the theme of truth is also present in every act of "faith in." A person who has faith in God inevitably also is convinced of the existence of God. A person who has faith in

Christ is also firmly convinced that Christ is God. To every "faith in" there corresponds not only a "faith that" the revelations of God are true but also a "faith that" the person in whom we have faith exists.

When, for example, we hear beautiful music and are deeply moved by it, our experience is certainly not a judgment about the beauty of the music. It is, rather, a direct contact with the beauty of the music, a being touched by the beauty and a responding with enthusiasm. But without any doubt, the statement "This music is beautiful" is implicitly held to be true. This is only a faint analogy, but it may suffice to suggest the manner in which every faith *in* implicitly contains a faith *that* the object of our faith exists. The person in whom I believe, to whom I surrender, is the absolute one. I believe that He is God, the epiphany of God. Important as it is, therefore, to distinguish the faith *in* from the faith *that*, important as it is to see that the former is the very basis of the latter, it is impossible to separate them in a way that would suggest that "faith in" could ever exist without "faith that." The two attitudes—the surrender to the person of Christ as God and the belief that Christ is the Son of God—are indeed different; but the faith *that* He is the Son of God is necessarily connected with the faith *in* Him. It is impossible for any faithful Christian not to believe that Christ is the Son of God. In Christ's question to His disciples, "Who do you say that I am?" and in St. Peter's answer, "Thou art the Christ, the Son of the Living God," the "faith that" is clearly present. And it is equally present in the sacerdotal prayer, "They have believed that Thou hast sent me." In both cases, let it be noted, the question of truth is fully present—truth, in the ultimate, all-embracing, inevitably presupposed meaning of the term. And this truth has no ambiguous "historical component."

It is also ambiguous to put forward the notion that biblical faith means that we follow Christ in our life. This is the thesis that Thomas Sartory puts forward amid all the confusion he generates in his playing with words. Now, it is certainly true that the living faith that Kierkegaard stresses implies our following Christ; it implies more than our conviction that what Christ has revealed is true; it implies a living of Christ in our soul, a continuously renewed giving of ourselves to Christ, and seeing everything in the light of Him. But faith, as such, which St. Paul clearly distinguishes from hope and charity, is nonetheless indissolubly connected with the conviction that Christ is the Son of God, the epiphany of God. In short, it is connected with the Divinity of Christ. To deny this very core of faith (of faith *that*, as well as of faith *in*) is to annihilate the faith to which the Gospel continually refers. When truth in its authentic sense plays no role in faith, faith has been lost. There is a glaring contradiction in the idea of Sartory and others that only "faith in Christ" and faithfulness to Him in our lives are absolute, and that every proposition that expresses something implicit in our faith is subject to historical evolution. This is a mere playing with words—which, incidentally, has become quite a fashionable way of solving problems since Heidegger.

The saints are the great witnesses of Christ and of the redemption of the world through Christ's death on the cross. They demonstrate the ineradicable connection of both "faith in" and "faith that" with the transformation of the personality in Christ. They truly realize the words of St. Paul: "I live, yet not I, but Christ lives in me." The lives of the saints exemplify the crucial importance of our following Christ, which includes love of God, love of neighbor, and the dwelling in the paths of the Lord—in one word, the realization of the entire natural and supernatural morality. To stress this is certainly in full conformity with the doctrine of the Church. It finds its classical expression in the Catholic doctrine of justification, which holds, against the Lutheran *sola fide* theory, that justification cannot be separated from sanctification and that only faith formed by charity (*fides caritate formata*) can lead to salvation. But this true following of Christ presupposes not only such a "faith in" but also the "faith that" of the Apostolic and Nicene Creeds. If it is erroneous to substitute the *sola fide* for the *fides caritate formata,* it is all the more so to substitute the imitation of Christ for faith; for the very basis of the imitation of Christ is faith in Christ. And this commitment to Christ cannot be separated from the firm belief that God exists, that Christ is the Son of the Living God. By this fact the full thematicity of truth in faith is disclosed. Thus, we see that the "biblical faith" advocated by Thomas Sartory and others is a completely ambiguous notion and leads to hopeless confusion. His "biblical faith" is neither the real "faith in" nor the real imitation and commitment that we witness in the saints.

The whole dissolution of truth is epitomized in the answer given by a theologian to the following question: "Did the Angel Gabriel really announce to the Virgin Mary the fact that she would give birth to Christ?" He answered, "This is an oriental truth." This answer implied that there are different types of truth, an oriental and an occidental, an old and a new. His juggling with the notion of truth reminds one of the distinctions made by the president of the Association of Mathematicians in National Socialist Germany between Jewish and Aryan mathematics.

When St. Augustine says, "What does our soul desire more than truth?" or when he exclaims, "Oh truth, truth, how did the very marrow of my bones yearn for thee," he is obviously referring to something over and above the truth of fundamental statements. Truth is envisaged as a whole, as one—as when we speak of the Kingdom of Truth. Here, as in the expression, "Truth shall make us free," the dignity and value of truth flashes forth. In this notion of truth as the splendor of light against darkness, of purity against impurity, of univocity against ambiguity, of clarity and articulation against chaos, the full dignity of being against non-being is present. We touch here on an ultimate datum that reaches into an unfathomable depth and mystery. The scope of this work does not permit us to pursue it, but we may quote the following passage from Guardini:

> Plato must have had an extraordinary experience of truth. For him, it is not merely the adequacy of a proposition, but an experience of truth with all its sublime import and plenitude of significance that the undistorted truth implies. For Plato, truth is not only the correctness and clarity of an insight; it is that sublime value which transcends the concrete content in every genuine knowledge.[3]

We come closer to this notion of truth if we consider the different gradations of weight and depth that the truth of a statement can assume, depending on whether it is of an insignificant, accidental nature or an important one. The content of propositions differs in many ways: important or unimportant, deep or superficial, intrinsically necessary or purely empirical. Though, as we saw, differences in content do not entitle us to speak of different types of truth, a truth nevertheless assumes a weight, status, and splendor according to the rank of the being in question. The splendor of a truth involving values is

3. Romano Guardini, *Stationen und Rückblicke* (Würzburg: Werkbund, 1965).

immeasurably greater than one that only deals with a neutral fact.

The higher the fact to which a truth refers, the more we can grasp the glorious value of truth. And yet, in every truth, even that of the most modest sentence, there is a reflection, however faint, of the glory of truth.

It is against this background that the words of Our Lord, "I am the truth," are to be understood. Here we are confronted with the one all-embracing truth, the Kingdom of Truth in all its liberating splendor—but in a completely new reality: truth as a person. The difference is analogous to that between justice and goodness and God's *being* infinite justice and goodness. The incomparably superior reality that personal being possesses over the impersonal is here apparent. In Christ we are confronted with Incarnate Truth, the Incarnate Word, in whom the overwhelming glory of the truth has an ultimate personal reality. As the truth that redeems us, that makes us free, Christ draws us into the Kingdom of Truth.

No twaddle about the difference between Greek and biblical truth can ever affect the fact that truth in all its dimensions is the backbone of Christian faith. Whether a person's faith is based on truth or error has an ultimate impact. In comparing the position of men like Thomas Sartory with that of Cardinal Newman or of any saint of the past, we are forced to conclude that many of the progressive Catholics have in reality lost their faith and are now trying desperately, by confused and pretentious constructs, to deceive both themselves and others about this dread fact.

FALSE FRONTS

At the National Socialist convention in Nuremberg, Minister Goebbels declared that only two great fronts still exist in the world today: the Bolshevist front, including all those who countenance Bolshevism; and the anti-Bolshevist, Fascist, and authoritarian front. National Socialism stands at the head of the second and has saved Germany from Bolshevism. Every conscientious person must therefore take his stance unequivocally in favor of the anti-Bolshevist front.

This essay was first published in German as "*Falsche Fronten*" in Hildebrand's anti-Nazi journal *Der christliche Ständestaat* on September 27, 1936. The English translation was made for *My Battle Against Hitler* (New York: Image Books, 2014), a book that presents for the first time in English many of Hildebrand's essays and actions that earned him the distinction of being the Nazi's "public enemy number one" in Vienna for his leadership of the intellectual resistance to Nazism.

Understandably, this rhetoric has made a great impression on many people. The terrible events in Spain, the assassination of the clergy and religious, and the destruction of precious cultural treasures have rightly led to reactions of terror and horror everywhere, and have made many aware of the fearful dynamic set in motion by the passions of the masses that have been unleashed.

We are not interested here in the question of how far Moscow can be held responsible for the events in Spain, nor whether the Spanish phenomenon is truly Bolshevism rather than anarchism. The Spanish atrocities were not needed in order to recognize the terrible nature of Bolshevism. Its materialistic ideology, its disregard for all personal freedom, its collectivism and anti-personalism, its mortal hatred of Christianity and indeed of all religion, are sufficient grounds for every true Catholic to reject it unambiguously and to oppose it unconditionally.

Nevertheless, the ideological division of the present-day world into Bolshevists and anti-Bolshevists that Goebbels proclaimed at the Nuremberg party convention is false. The real battle lines drawn at the level of ideas are, in fact, very different. I have often pointed out in these pages that there is only one real antithesis to all errors, namely, truth itself. For errors, no matter how different they may be among themselves, are not truly antithetical to one another. Traditionalism and ontologism, Pelagianism and the Protestant doctrine of *sola fide* (by faith alone), collectivism and liberal individualism, socialism and capitalism—these pairs do tend in opposite directions, but because one error never counteracts what is specifically false in another, opposite error, none of them constitutes a genuine antithesis. In every case, the two are fundamentally related; they both proceed from the same initial falsehood, even though they move in opposite directions. Only the one truth opposes all errors, whatever their nature, both in their most decisive point and in their specific disvalue. One error can never be overcome by another, opposite error; the devil cannot be cast out with the help of Beelzebub.

In reality, there have been only two fronts in the world for the past two thousand years: the front for Christ and the front against Christ. He is the cornerstone which separates all spirits. All other antitheses bypass the decisive question and thus remain superficial.

The question "for or against Christ" can be

understood either in a more specifically religious sense or in a broader cultural and intellectual sense. In the former case, the question of the true Christian faith is the criterion of being for or against Christ; in the latter, it is the question of how much someone still holds fast to the foundations of the Christian West in a moral, legal, sociological, and cultural sense.

The contemporary intellectual crisis in Europe divides people into two camps: the enemies of Christian Western culture and those who somehow still hold on (in greatly varying degrees) to the foundations of this culture. The latter group may also include those who cannot be designated as Christians in a religious sense.

So what, then, defines the Christian West in this broader cultural and intellectual sense? In what respect does the Christian West form the real front against both Nazism and Communism? The first decisive element is the stance toward the question of truth. A profound reverence for truth is an integral aspect of Christian Western culture, as is a clear consciousness that the question of truth stands at the beginning of all decisions and cannot in any way be subordinated to practical considerations.

The view that [German] Minister of Culture Schemm expressed in an address to professors of the University of Munich in 1933 is diametrically opposed to this reverence for the question of truth: "From now on, what matters for you is not to ascertain whether something is true, but rather whether it is in line with the National Socialist revolution." The same holds for the following words in the National Socialist program: "We confess allegiance to Christianity insofar as it is in keeping with the Germanic racial sensibility." Here, the decisive question is no longer whether the doctrine of Christianity is objectively true, but whether it is in keeping with the subjective sensibility of a race and conforms to a certain racial ethos.

It must be noted that this attitude is much more radically opposed to the spirit of Christianity than the typical form of atheism, for the latter acknowledges, at least in principle, the decisive role of the question of truth. In National Socialism, however, the question of truth as such is suppressed in favor of a purely subjective factor. The question of the truth or falsity of a worldview, which alone should be decisive for our positive or negative response to it, is deposed from its seat of judgment. This connotes a still deeper breach with any adherence to objective truth than is to be found even in radical skepticism. When the latter denies the existence of objective truth, it necessarily takes seriously the question of truth as such. Here, however, the question of truth has been trivialized. The faculty for discerning the seriousness of the question of truth has died; the interest in the elementary question "What is true?" has been extinguished. This signifies an irrevocable break with the whole of Christian Western culture, which rests on the foundation of reverence for truth.

A second foundational element of Christian Western culture is the conviction that there is an objective moral law which is independent of all subjective interests, arbitrariness, and mere power. Whether committed by individual rulers or democratic masses, breaches of the law have always occurred *de facto* in the history of the West. But there has always been some adherence to the idea of an objective law and the question of right has been regarded as independent of the sheer assertion of anyone's egoistic wishes. This belief in an objective law immune to the arbitrariness of individuals and nations is an inheritance of the Christian worldview, which is still preserved even by many enemies of

Christianity (although this is illogical from a strictly religious point of view) and also underlies the concept of the League of Nations.

The frequently repeated declaration of the National Socialist leaders that there is no objective right or wrong, and that "what is right is what is useful for the German people," fundamentally breaks with this foundational element of the public life of the Christian West. The path for this National Socialist doctrine was prepared in the realm of philosophical theory by various forms of relativism and positivism, but only National Socialism has dared to draw out its basic consequence in praxis—that is, the conscious, programmatic renunciation of the foundation expressed in the words *iustitia fundamentum regnorum* (justice is the foundation of states).

Here too, an unbridgeable abyss opens up. On the one side stand all those who still hold fast to an objective law and believe that in individual cases of conflict, the question of right ought to take precedence over the question of sheer power; on the other stand all those who deny any such objective law in principle. It is absolutely impossible for these two sides to reach an understanding or meet on common ground. In cases of conflict, they cannot even appeal to a purely timeless, objective norm on the basis of which a decision could be made, for the one side denies that there is any authority higher than its own naked interests. We must not underestimate the depth of this difference, for here all spirits definitively part ways. With the denial of an objective law one not only stands outside Christianity as a religion but also outside the entire classical and humane cultural tradition of the West, which has received its decisive formation from Christianity.

A third fundamental element of Christian Western culture is the primacy of the spiritual sphere over the vital and, *a fortiori*, over mere matter. The divinely ordained hierarchy of the spheres of being has been denied by many philosophical systems, but Soviet Russia and the Third Reich were the first to deny this hierarchy in their official state ideologies and to draw the consequences of this denial in their laws and in the way they educate their youth. In Christian Western culture, the spiritual sphere is held to be higher than the vital and purely material spheres, the latter of which were bound to serve the former.

It is also considered to be ontologically superior. This position finds its classical expression in the wonderful words of St. Thomas: *anima forma corporis* (the soul is the form of the body). The composition of a person's blood is not decisive for his spirit; as a spiritual person, man proceeds directly from the hand of God, and his free will, his education, and his openness to the workings of grace play the decisive role in his development. Health is certainly a value, but what is it when compared with high intellectual gifts, to moral or religious values? Geniuses who were pitiful figures from a vital perspective have often kindled people's enthusiasm—and great intellects were so often such small, frail, and sickly men from a vital point of view. When a person possessed great intellectual capacities despite his deficiencies in the vital sphere, people grasped the tremendous victory of the spirit that he embodied. Two examples would be Kant and Prince Eugene; the latter, as is generally known, was physically deformed.

Both economic materialism, in which all spiritual values are merely a means to an end, and racial materialism, which idolizes the vital sphere, break in principle with this self-evident primacy of the spirit. The laws governing sterilization and marriage in the Third Reich and, above all, its racial doctrine—which reduces the individual spiritual person to a mere product of race—are clear expressions of a radical breach with this cornerstone of Christian Western culture.

A fourth factor—perhaps the most decisive of all—is connected with this last point. Since the Renaissance, various liberal theories have stripped the human person of his true nobility as the image of God. First, immortality was denied to the person, then freedom of will, then the capacity to make meaningful, intentional responses. Some saw the human being as a bundle of meaningless sensations, others saw him as a more highly developed animal. The practical consequences of this devaluation of the person were never drawn. A certain reverence for the dignity of the person, his inalienable rights, and his freedom of opinion lived on, though in reality such things logically presuppose the Christian concept of the human person.

It was left to Bolshevism and National Socialism to draw the ultimate consequences of this devaluation of the human person and to develop an antipersonalism which is radically opposed to Christianity. Here, the essential point is not whether the person is held to be a mere means for the state, the nation, a racial community, or an economic collective.

What *is* decisive is the collectivism that subordinates the person in his very being and value to some natural community. According to the Christian conception, every human being has an immortal soul destined to be a vessel of grace and to enjoy eternal communion with God, which therefore possesses a higher value than anything else on earth. The fate of states, nations, and peoples as such is incomparably less important than the eternal salvation of a single immortal soul.

It is here most of all—in the position one takes toward the individual—that thinkers part ways. Anyone who advocates this anti-personalism has drawn the ultimate consequence of his breach with Christianity and has joined the irreconcilable enemies of Christian Western culture. Anyone who still holds fast to genuine reverence for the individual person is in some way drawing, albeit unconsciously, from Christian thought.

Closely connected with this is one's attitude toward the poor, the sick, and the weak. Christ says: "As you did it to one of the least of these my brethren, you did it to me" (Matthew 25:40). The National Socialist morality of the master race views the sick and the weak as "faulty products" who are a tiresome burden on human society. The "hero ethos" of National Socialism and the ethos of the Sermon on the Mount constitute an utter antithesis. It is futile to attempt to combine them in any way; a choice must be made between these two worlds—separated, as they are, by an unbridgeable abyss.

If we take our starting point from these decisive philosophical antitheses in the contemporary political-social-cultural crisis, it becomes clear that the true demarcation of fronts turns out to be quite different from what the National Socialist party convention in Nuremberg would have us think. Purely political interests and exclusively tactical deliberations may lead to the formation of certain groupings, but the fronts that are based on worldviews—which will, in the long run, prove to be decisive in the political realm as well—are definitively sundered according to whether they make a radical break with the entirety of Christian Western culture or adhere to it, at least in its essential foundations.

The ideological distinction between Bolshevism and National Socialism is not so very great, despite all the violent political animosity between them, which has totally different roots. One person might want to make an ally of Bolshevism while another may want an alliance with National Socialism, but the Catholic is separated from both by an unbridgeable abyss. He cannot choose between them, because they are essentially united on those critical points that separate them decisively from Christianity. All he can do is oppose both, pointing to Christ and the foundations of Christian Western culture, which alone constitute their true antithesis. He must see these ideologies as two equally dangerous, irreconcilable enemies of Christ.

www.ingramcontent.com/pod-product-compliance
Lightning Source LLC
LaVergne TN
.VHW020048110826
45155LV00029B/689